ANCIENT CIVILIZATIONS

Rome

By Christy Steele

Steadwell
Books

Raintree Steck-Vaughn Publishers
A Harcourt Company

Austin · New York
www.steck-vaughn.com

Published by Raintree Steck-Vaughn Publishers, an imprint of Steck-Vaughn Company.

Library of Congress Cataloging-in-Publication Data
Cataloging-in-Publication data is available upon request.

Produced by Compass Books

Photo Acknowledgments
Corbis, cover; Archivo Iconografico, 9; Araldo de Luca, 10, 25, 26; Mimmo Jodice, 12, 14, 19; Vanni Archive, 16; Bettmann, 20; Massimo Listri, 22 Root Resources, 32; Kenneth Rapalee, 29, 47
Visuals Unlimited, 30, 34; Charles Preitner, 37; K. Collins, 38; Ann B. Swengel, 41; Hal Beral, 42

Content Consultants
Sherwin Little
Vice President
American Classical League

Julie Langford-Johnson
Associate Instructor
Department of Classical Studies
Indiana University

Don L. Curry
Educational Author, Editor, Consultant, and Columnist

Contents

Atlantic
Ocean

LEGEND

☐ Ancient Rome

☐ Surrounding Land

☐ Mountains

● Cities

⟨ Rivers

☐ Water

BRITAIN
London

GERMANY

E U R O P E

Rhine
River

GAUL

Danube River

Alps

PANNONIA

DACIA

Bla
Se

Adriatic
Sea

Constantinople

SPAIN

CORSICA

Rome
ITALY

Pompeii

MACEDONIA

SARDINIA

Naples

GREECE

Aegean
Sea

SICILY

Ionian
Sea

Athens

Carthage

CRETE

Mediterranean
Sea

A F R I C A

Roman History

Ancient Romans created a **civilization** that lasted for more than 1,000 years (753 B.C. to A.D. 476). Ancient means old. During that time, the Roman people formed a great civilization. A civilization is an advanced **society**. A society shares a common way of life.

Roman society worked well. Latin was the main language of Rome. People paid taxes and obeyed the laws of Roman government.

Romans took over many other countries and made them a part of their **empire**. An empire is a group of countries that all have the same ruler. At its most powerful, Rome controlled many countries, including most of Europe, Greece, Egypt, and parts of Asia.

ROMAN TIMELINE

800-700 BC	Italy inhabited by Hellenic and Etruscan people.
753 BC	Romulus founds Roman culture at the Palatine.
524 BC	Greeks stop the southward Etruscan migration at Cumae.
509 BC	Romans overthrow tyrant Tarquinius Superbus, ending the Etruscan dynasty.
450 BC	Twelve Tables of Roman law are published.
396 BC	The city of Veii is conquered.
340 BC	The Latin War begins.
264 BC	First Punic War to take Carthage for dominance of Mediterranean.
241 BC	Romans win Sicily.
221 BC	The structure Circus Flaminius is built.
218-201 BC	Second Punic War brings the defeat of General Hannibal of Carthage.
179 BC	The structure Basilica Aemilia is built.
149-146 BC	Third Punic War ends with the Roman capture of Carthage.
44 BC	The assassination of Julius Caesar ends the Roman Republic.
31 BC	Octavian Caesar defeats Mark Antony and becomes emperor of Roman world. He is given title Augustus.
14 BC	Augustus dies.
41 AD	Gaius Julius, the emperor Caligula, is murdered.
43 AD	Claudius wins victories in Britain.
64 AD	Rome is burnt.

Roman Beginnings

The Age of the Seven Kings was the earliest part of Roman history. During this time, kings ruled from the city of Rome. According to ancient Roman stories, a man named Romulus started Rome in 753 B.C. on seven hills surrounding the Tiber River.

6

Several tribes lived in Rome. A tribe is a large group of families that share the same way of life. A tribe called the Latins took over Italy and made Rome their capital. A capital is a city that is the center of government.

The Age of the Republic was the second part of Roman history. It started when Romans fought against their king in 509 B.C. They threw the king out of Rome and set up a **republic**. A republic is a form of government where people choose their rulers by voting. The Age of the Republic started to end when the leader Julius Caesar was killed in 44 B.C. After he died, Romans fought each other to gain power.

The Age of Emperors was the third and last part of Roman history. It started in 27 B.C. when Octavius, Caesar's grandnephew and adopted son, became **emperor** of Rome. An emperor is the ruler of an empire. Emperors were like kings. They made new laws and tax rules. They built new cities. They went to war and took over new places and people.

The Government

At first, only free rich men in the city of Rome could become **citizens**. A citizen could own property, vote, and serve in the government and the army. A citizen's job was also to work to make Rome better. Many rich citizens paid for buildings and roads in their towns. After A.D. 212, free men from all over the Roman Empire could become citizens. But women and slaves were never allowed to become citizens.

Rome changed its form of government several times during its history. During the Age of the Republic, the Senate was the main power in Rome. The Senate was a group of citizens chosen to run the government.

Each year, Roman citizens voted for two people to head the Senate. These two men were called consuls. Consuls ran the Roman army, Senate meetings, and the government.

During the Age of Emperors, the emperor ran the government and ruled the army. The Senate did not have much power.

This painting shows a Roman senator giving a speech.

Ruling foreign lands was also important to the Roman Empire. Romans called foreign lands provinces. The emperor placed a legatus in charge of each province. The legatus was a governor. The legatus controlled the Roman army in his province. He had many helpers called tribunes.

 This painting from an ancient Roman wall shows the clothing of a legionnaire.

Roman Army

Rome became a great empire because of its army. The army fought Roman enemies, took over new places, and brought slaves back to Rome. The army also helped rulers keep peace. Emperors could not rule without help from the army. Sometimes the army would take an emperor out of power and make a favorite general the emperor.

At its largest, nearly one-half million men served in the Roman army. Soldiers served in the army for 20 to 25 years. Rome paid its soldiers. The soldiers used this money to pay for their food, armor, and weapons. Armor is metal coverings worn by soldiers to keep them safe when they fight. Weapons are tools used for fighting.

Most members of the army were Roman-citizen foot soldiers called legionnairies. Each carried a sword, two javelins, and a shield. A javelin is a light spear that can be thrown. Legionnairies wore armor and carried shields to protect their bodies. They also wore helmets to keep their heads safe.

Auxiliaries were slaves or non-Roman foot soldiers. After serving in the army, they were often given Roman citizenship.

A centurion was a soldier in charge of 100 legionnairies. The tribunes and the legatus were in charge of the centurions.

This patrician mother is teaching the alphabet to her child.

Daily Life in Rome

There were three groups of Roman citizens. People were in groups based on their family, job, and their money and property.

Patricians were Romans of the highest ruling class. Patrician families often had a great deal of money and power. They held important jobs in government or the church. Most emperors, senators, and consuls were patricians.

Equites were Romans of the middle class. Equites were mostly rich businesspeople. They were traders, bankers, and tax collectors.

Plebeians were Romans of the lower class. Plebeians were farmers, craftspeople, and shop owners. Plebeians did not have much power, but they voted for their rulers.

Each household had a special place like this where the paterfamilias gave offerings to the household gods.

The Roman Family

The family was important to the Roman way of life. A paterfamilias, or father, ruled his family until he died. He controlled all of the people in his household, including his wife, the children, and slaves. The father made offerings to the household gods and goddesses.

The paterfamilias had a great deal of power over his children. Throughout their lives, he decided whether they would live or die. He decided what jobs the children would do. When they were grown, the paterfamilias picked husbands or wives for his children. Some girls married as early as age 12. Boys were several years older before they got married. The paterfamilias kept controlling his children, even after they were married and had children of their own.

The paterfamilias usually left the running of the household to his wife. If the family had slaves, she made sure the family's slaves cleaned the house. She made cloth. She also decided what the household would eat and wear. Women in Rome could not be a part of government. Most rich women did not have jobs outside of the home. But poor women sometimes had jobs. Some worked as doctors. Others helped their husbands work.

This photograph shows a peristyle in the remains of a Roman house.

Roman Homes

Rich Romans and poor Romans lived in very different kinds of houses. Poor Romans in cities often lived in large blocks of apartments. These apartments were called insulae. Insulae were built mainly of wood.

Insulae had up to seven floors. The first floor often had small shops that sold food and other goods. It also had public bathrooms. Large apartments filled the lower floors. Small apartments filled the upper floors. The apartments usually had no kitchens, running water, or bathrooms.

Rich Romans often had two houses. One house was in the country and one in the city. Each house had one or two floors. Romans usually built a wall around their houses.

Roman houses were built around one or two indoor courtyards called atriums. Pools to catch rainwater for drinking were often in the center. Most houses also had an open garden called a peristyle. A roofed walkway supported by tall columns surrounded the peristyle. Pools and fountains were often in the peristyle.

Romans built the other rooms of the house around atriums and peristyles. Bedrooms, dining rooms, and the kitchen opened onto these spaces. They also had a place where the paterfamilias made offerings to household gods.

Roman Clothes

Weather in many parts of the Roman Empire was often hot. Roman clothes were simple and cool. Most Roman clothes were loose-fitting so that air could flow around people's bodies and help keep them cool.

Most men, women, and children wore tunics. A tunic is a long, straight, loose-fitting piece of clothing. Tunics could have short sleeves or no sleeves. They could be different lengths. Most men wore knee-length tunics. Women wore longer tunics.

People often wore other clothing over their tunics. Male Roman citizens wore togas. A toga was a piece of cloth draped over the arm and shoulders. It could be more than 18 feet (5.5 m) long. Most citizens wore white togas. In Rome, purple was a special color that stood for power. Only the most powerful people in Rome could wear purple. Only emperors could wear purple togas.

Ancient Romans dressed in their finest
clothes to attend music performances.

A married woman sometimes wore a dress
called a stola over the tunic. A stola was long
and came to a woman's ankles. It was
gathered in two different places, under the
chest and the hips.

▲ This stone carving shows an early Roman school. Students sat around their teachers.

Roman Education

Early Rome had no schools. Rich parents hired teachers or bought educated slaves to teach their children. Poor parents taught their children whatever they could. Fathers taught boys how to read, write, hunt, and fight. Mothers sometimes taught their children letters and numbers. They also taught girls household jobs, such as how to cook, clean, and make cloth.

Later, some teachers started schools in their homes. Rich parents paid for their sons to attend these schools. Poor parents could not afford to send their children to school. Most girls did not attend schools.

Students started school at age seven. Young students learned how to read and write the Latin **alphabet** and Roman numerals. They wrote with a **stylus** on small wood pieces that were covered with wax. A stylus is a tool with one pointed end and one flat end. Students wrote letters or numbers in the wax with the pointed end. They used the flat end to rub out the letters or mistakes. When they were 11, students studied Greek and Latin poetry and other famous books.

Rich students who wanted government jobs continued schooling. They learned Roman law and practiced giving speeches. Sometimes they went on a trip around the empire.

Virgil was a famous Roman poet. He wrote the *Aeneid* about a Greek hero.

Roman Culture

A group of people's ideas, customs, traditions, and way of life make up their **culture**. Roman people showed what they were like through the things they made. Romans thought their way of life was the best. So, they built new Roman buildings and cities in the places they took over.

Roman culture spread throughout the lands they took over. Many people throughout the Roman Empire learned Latin. They wrote plays and books in this common language. Some of Rome's famous writers were Cicero, Virgil, and Pliny the Elder. They wrote about history, heroes, the gods and goddesses, and science.

Roman Religion

Religion was an important part of Roman culture. Religion is belief and worship in a god or gods. Roman people had many different gods and goddesses. They believed that each god or goddess was in charge of a different thing. For example, Mars was the Roman god of war.

Romans began worshiping new gods whenever they added another country to their empire. For example, the Romans worshiped many of the Greek and Egyptian gods and goddesses when they took over those places.

Romans built special buildings, called temples, where priests worshiped and served the gods. The Romans gave offerings of money, food, and other things to their gods and goddesses. They hoped that the gods would be pleased by the offerings.

At certain times of the year, Romans held celebrations to honor the gods and goddesses. In Rome, these were holy days.

This is a statue of Jupiter, the Roman king of the gods.

People did not work. The Roman government held races, games, and shows for the people.

Often people in different parts of the Roman Empire worshiped their own gods. Each household also worshiped their own gods. Household gods were often spirits of dead family members.

This mosaic of sea creatures was on the floor of an ancient Roman house.

Roman Art

Roman rulers wanted works of art to send important messages. Rulers or rich people hired artists to create scenes that showed battles that they had won. They had artists paint pictures showing how wonderful Roman life was. Emperors also hired artists to make statues of them. The rulers put these works of art in public places in Rome and other countries in the Roman Empire.

Roman artists were especially good at making portraits. A portrait is a picture or drawing of a person. Roman artists tried to paint or sculpt objects as they looked in real life. Artists from other countries often tried to make people look better than they really did. Roman artists also copied works done by some Greek artists.

A great deal of Roman art was religious. Roman artists carved statues of the gods and goddesses out of stone, such as marble. They also painted or carved pictures of the gods and goddesses on the walls and ceilings of temples and other public buildings.

Rich people bought art for their houses. Artists painted scenes that covered whole rooms of the houses. They hired artists to make floor **mosaics**. A mosaic is a picture or design made with small pieces of colored tile, glass, or stone.

Roman Architecture

Romans built large, beautiful buildings to show people how powerful Rome was. Romans copied some of the Greek **architecture**. Architecture is the look and way a building is made. Like the Greeks, many Roman public buildings had columns.

Unlike the Greeks, Romans used domes and **arches** in their buildings. A dome is a rounded roof. An arch forms the upper edge of an open space and supports the weight of the building above it. An arch can be curved, pointed, or flat. Besides buildings, Romans used arches in doorways and bridges. They also built special large arches over roadways. These arches were so large that people could walk or ride horses through the arches. Rulers often built these arches after winning a war or coming into power. Artists put writing or pictures of the special event on the arch.

The Romans thought of better ways to make buildings. They invented **concrete**. Concrete is a strong construction material.

Roman temples often have many columns.
This is the Temple of Neptune.

Romans mixed sand, stone, and water to
make concrete. They used concrete to build
huge buildings with many floors, such as the
Circus Maximus. The Circus Maximus was a
huge racetrack in Rome. About 250,000
people could sit there.

The ruins of the Roman city Pompeii show how it is set up in square blocks.

Roman Cities

Except for Rome, most Roman cities were set up the same way. Each city was set up like a checkerboard. It had a series of square blocks. Roads were straight. They either traveled north to south or west to east.

A **forum** was a large open courtyard in the center of a Roman city. Romans used the forum to hold large meetings or celebrations. They also met friends and discussed business there.

Around the edges of the forum, Romans built important public buildings. These included temples and government buildings, such as a town hall and a courthouse.

Sometimes public baths were also around the forum. A bath was a huge building with many different rooms. Some had libraries, gardens, rooms for exercising, and rooms with large pools for bathing. Baths were the social center of Roman life.

A large marketplace was also near the forum. A marketplace was an area full of small shops. Each shop sold something different, such as food, clothes, jewelry, or **pottery**.

Many large towns also had a half-circle shaped theater and an oval-shaped theater called an amphitheater. Actors performed plays in theaters. Fighters called gladiators fought for sport in amphitheaters.

Because Romans built so many roads, ancient people had a saying, "all roads lead to Rome."

What Did the Romans Do?

One of Rome's greatest acts was building roads. The Roman army built many roads. Roads were built in a straight line to carry things from one place to another quickly.

First, workers dug a hole where the road was going to be built. They filled the bottom layer with sand. Then, they filled the next layer with large stone pieces mixed with cement. This layer was covered with crushed stone mixed with cement. Finally, workers laid large stone blocks on top of the road.

By the end of the Roman Empire, Romans had built more than 55,000 miles (88,514 km) of roads. Many modern roads were built on top of these early Roman roads.

Ancient Romans built this aqueduct in Spain.

Roman Discoveries

Roman discoveries were useful. A discovery is something that is found out. Roman inventions were mainly things that people needed to live well.

Romans invented new ways to heat buildings. They made buildings with raised floors and empty space between the walls. Heat from wood fires flowed under the floors and through hollow bricks in the walls. This heated the floors and the air in the rooms above them.

Romans also invented ways to carry water. They built many stone and concrete **aqueducts**. An aqueduct is a pipe or channel built to carry water from one place to another. Aqueducts brought water from mountain springs into cities and towns. Some aqueducts were built above the ground and were supported by huge arches. Other aqueducts were underground. Without aqueducts, people in cities would not have had enough water.

Romans also built large sewers in their cities. Waste flowed into special aqueducts that carried it out of the city. This helped keep the water and the city cleaner.

Fall of Rome

The Roman Empire kept growing larger throughout the Age of Emperors. It reached its largest when Emperor Trajan ruled. At this point, the empire covered about 2.5 million square miles (6.5 million square km).

Hadrian was emperor after Trajan. He stopped the spread of the empire. He also let some faraway countries leave the empire. It was too costly to fight to keep these places.

Over the next 200 years, Rome began falling apart. Roman generals fought against each other for power. In A.D. 285, Emperor Diocletian split the empire into two parts. Each part had its own emperor. The capital of the Western Empire was Rome. The capital of the Eastern Empire was Constantinople. This city is now called Istanbul, Turkey.

Different countries began fighting Rome. They wanted to rule Rome. The Roman army was not strong enough to fight all its enemies. In A.D. 476, the Germans removed

Today, the remains of Roman buildings are still standing in Turkey.

the last western Roman emperor from power. People use this date as the end of the Roman Empire. The Eastern Empire lasted for another 1,000 years. But in A.D. 1453, the Turks took over Constantinople. At this time, the Eastern Empire ended.

This ancient Roman coin has a portrait of Emperor Trajan on it.

How We Know about Rome

People today know about Rome because of the history books, letters, and poems that they wrote. **Archaeology** also shows much about the Romans. Archaeology is the study of ancient remains. Archaeologists study objects made by ancient Romans. The objects show what life was like during that time.

People have found many Roman **artifacts**. An artifact is an object that was made or used by humans in the past. Some artifacts are Roman coins. They often had portraits of leaders on them. Statues and pictures show how Romans dressed and what they looked like.

Pompeii and Herculaneum

Archaeologists know about Roman life by studying the remains of Roman buildings. Archaeologists have learned the most about ancient Rome by digging up the Roman towns of Pompeii and Herculaneum. The volcano Mount Vesuvius blew out ash and mud in A.D. 70. The ash and mud buried these towns. The towns are full of buildings and artifacts that show what daily life in ancient Rome was like.

Archaeologists study Roman writing and carvings found in the towns. Romans wrote poems on the walls for the people they loved. Businesspeople kept records of taxes and how much money people owed. Even some letters and books were found buried. Archaeologists can read these things to learn more about marriage, children, and laws of the time.

Mosaics and paintings picture Roman life. Some mosaics show Romans lying down on couches while they ate. They show Romans

drinking wine and eating grapes and other foods. They show performers dancing, singing, or acting. Other paintings show scenes from Roman baths or slaves combing the hair of rich people. Still other carvings show how the army fought Rome's enemies.

People often visit the Pantheon, one of the most famous Roman temples.

Rome in the Modern World

Roman ideas still shape the world today. For example, the Roman government wrote down their laws. This set of laws was called the 12 Tables. Many countries set up their country's laws like the Romans did. France based its set of laws on the 12 Tables. Many students in law schools around the world must still study the 12 Tables.

Roman ways of building are still useful. Most modern buildings and roads are made with concrete. Today, the look of Roman architecture is called "the classical style." People build many classical buildings with columns, domes, and arches.

The Latin language of the Romans is still used today. For thousands of years, writers used Latin to write most of the important history and science books. The modern alphabet of many languages was based on the Latin alphabet. Many words people use today come from the Latin language. Most months of the year came from Latin words. Many planets were named after Roman gods and goddesses.

Many people today are still interested in ancient Rome. Some people learn Latin. Other people visit the remains of ancient Roman places. These remains remind people of the power and beauty of ancient Rome.

Glossary

alphabet (AL-fuh-bet)—all the letters of a language arranged in order

aqueduct (AK-wuh-duhkt)—a pipe or channel built to carry water from one place to another

arch (ARCH)—a curved structure; an arch often helps support a building or a bridge.

archaeology (ar-kee-OL-uh-jee)—the study of ancient remains

architecture (AR-ki-tek-chur)—the look and way a building is made

artifact (ART-uh-fakt)—an object that was made or used by humans in the past

citizen (SIT-I-zuhn)—a member of a country who has rights under the law

civilization (siv-i-luh-ZAY-shuhn)—a highly developed and organized society

concrete (KON-kreet)—a building material made from a mixture of sand, gravel, cement, and water

culture (KUHL-chur)—the way of life, ideas, customs, and traditions of a group of people

emperor (EM-pur-ur)—the ruler of an empire, most often a man

empire (EM-pire)—a group of countries with one ruler

forum (FOR-uhm)—the open courtyard in the center of an ancient Roman city

mosaic (moh-ZAY-ik)—a pattern or picture made up of small pieces of colored stone, tile, or glass

pottery (POT-ur-ee)—objects made of baked clay

republic (ri-PUHB-lik)— a form of government where people choose their rulers by voting

society (suh-SYE-uh-tee)—a group of people with a common way of life

stylus (STEYE-luhs)—a tool with a pointed end and a flat end that is used for writing

Internet Sites

Ancient Rome Daily Life
http://members.aol.com/Donnclass/Romelife.
html

The Electronic Passport to Rome
http://www.mrdowling.com/702rome.html

Virtual Walking Tours of Ancient Rome
http://www.ancientsites.com/as/rome/academy
/tours/

Voyage Back in Time: Ancient Greece and Rome
http://www.richmond.edu/~ed344/webunits/
greecerome/

Useful Addresses

American Classical League
Miami University
Oxford, OH 45056-1694

**Classical Association of the Middle West
  and South**
Department of Classics
Randolph-Macon College
Ashland, VA 23005

 **This statue of Julius Caesar stands in an arch
on an ancient Roman building.**

Index

aqueduct, 35
army, 8, 9, 10-11, 33, 36, 41
atrium, 17

baths, 31, 41

Caesar, Julius, 7
centurion, 11
citizen, 8, 11, 13, 18
concrete, 28-29, 35, 43
consul, 8, 13

equite, 13

gladiator, 31

insulae, 16-17

Latin, 5, 21, 23, 43
legatus, 9, 11

legionnairies, 11

mosaic, 27, 40

paterfamilias, 14, 15, 17
patrician, 13
peristyle, 17
plebeians, 13
Pompeii, 40-41
portrait, 27, 39

roads, 8, 33
Romulus, 6

Senate, 8
stola, 19
stylus, 21

toga, 18
tribune, 9, 11
tunic, 18